Native American Art of the Northwest Coast

Celeste Bishop

INFOMAX COMMON CORE READERS

Rosen Classroom™

New York

Published in 2014 by The Rosen Publishing Group, Inc.
29 East 21st Street, New York, NY 10010

Book Design: Katelyn Londino

Photo Credits: Cover JJ Studio/Shutterstock.com; pp. 3–24 (border) Radiocat/Shutterstock.com; p. 5 (main) Rigucci/Shutterstock.com; pp. 5, 22 (map) Ridvan EFE/Shutterstock.com; pp. 7, 22 (house post) Richard Cummins/Lonely Planet Images/Getty Images; p. 7 (outdoor totem pole) steve estvanik/Shutterstock.com; p. 9 Max Lindenthaler/Shutterstock.com; p. 11 Melville B. Grosvenor/National Geographic/Getty Images; pp. 13, 22 (transformation mask) Canadian School/The Bridgeman Art Library/Getty Images; pp. 15, 22 (Tlingit robe) Joel Bennett/Peter Arnold/Getty Images; p. 17 (left) en.wikipedia.org/wiki/File:Thuja_plicata_Vancouver.jpg/Wikipedia.org; p. 17 (right) en.wikipedia.org/wiki/File:Moa-4.jpg/Wikipedia.org; p. 19 Marilyn Angel Wynn/Nativestock/Getty Images; p. 21 John Elk/Lonely Planet Images/Getty Images; p. 22 (baskets) lynnette/Shutterstock.com; p. 22 (argillite carving) en.wikipedia.org/wiki/File:Haida_argillite_carving_BC_1850_nmai13-1875.jpg/Wikipedia.org.

ISBN: 978-1-4777-2652-5
6-pack ISBN: 978-1-4777-2653-2

Manufactured in the United States of America

CPSIA Compliance Information: Batch #CS13RC: For further information contact Rosen Publishing, New York, New York at 1-800-237-9932.

Contents

Grandma's Collection

My grandma has a collection of art at her house. She likes to collect art from the Northwest Coast of North America. She has art from Native American tribes in Oregon, Washington, Alaska, and Canada. Grandma says the art a tribe creates is a very important part of who they are.

Northwest Coast tribes are known for making totem poles. My grandma says that's not all they make! I want to learn as much as I can about the art of these tribes. That way, I'll understand more about their **culture**.

The Northwest Coast has a lot of water and forests. Some of the tribes found there are the Tlingit (TLING-kuht), Haida (HY-duh), Salish (SAY-lihsh), and Tsimshian (CHIHM-shee-uhn).

Alaska

Washington

Oregon

Canada

United States

■ Northwest Coast (U.S.)
■ Northwest Coast (Canada)

5

Special Monuments

Totem poles are monuments carved to honor something or someone. They're carved to look like animals and people stacked one on top of another. The figures tell a story about an event, person, family, or community.

Grandma says most tribes make totem poles from the wood of the red cedar tree. Totem poles are usually around 10 to 60 feet (3 to 18 m) tall, but some are 100 feet (30 m) or taller! Some totem poles stand free, while others are house posts.

All totem poles are different. The Salish tribe preferred house posts, while the Haida tribe preferred tall totem poles outside.

Salish house post

Haida totem pole

I notice that most totem poles have animals on them. Grandma says totem poles can tell history because a figure can **represent** something else. An eagle might represent one family, while a bear might represent another. If these families came together in history, their totem pole might have a bear and an eagle on it.

Totem poles are sometimes made when people die to honor what they did in life. Other totem poles may tell the history of a community or its **folklore**. They're reminders of important things that happened.

Some common animals on totem poles are bears, frogs, whales, wolves, and ravens.

Different Masks

My grandma has a few masks in her art collection. She has an owl, an eagle, and a frog mask. Masks like these are made for people to buy, but they're also made for more important reasons.

It's a **tradition** for dancers to wear these masks during ceremonies, or special occasions. Masks **transform** a dancer into something or someone else. In the past, some ceremonies honored the hunting season. People believed that by dancing and wearing animal masks, they would have a successful hunt.

Even today, Northwest Coast Native Americans are trained as dancers so they can be a part of traditional ceremonies.

My grandma tells me about transformation masks. These masks have two faces, with one underneath the other. The outside mask is often an animal, and the inside mask is a person. Other masks have two humanlike faces. There are strings that allow the mask to be opened and closed.

Transformation masks show that people and animals can take different forms. They're sometimes worn during ceremonies, especially during dances. They represent tribal beliefs that living things can transform from one bodily form to another.

This is a transformation mask from the Kwakiutl (kwah-kee-YOO-tuhl) tribe. There's an eagle on the outside and a man on the inside.

13

Robes, Baskets, and More!

The tribes of the Northwest Coast make more than just masks and totem poles! Grandma collects argillite carvings, which are commonly made by the Haida tribe. These are figures made from argillite, which is a kind of black slate.

Grandma also has a Chilkat robe, which is a Tlingit art. Tlingits weave cedar bark and wool together to make beautiful robes of many colors.

Next, Grandma wants to buy Northwest Coast baskets. They're made of roots, bark, and grass. People use them to gather and store food.

There are so many different kinds of tribal art.
My favorite is the Chilkat robe because it's so colorful!

How They Lived

Grandma reminds me that art tells a lot about how people live. I learn that the Northwest Coast tribes have very close communities. Tribes used to live in longhouses, which were buildings that could hold many families. Longhouses were made from red cedar.

I noticed that tribes also used red cedar to make Chilkat robes and totem poles. Grandma says that red cedar is very important to Northwest Coast tribes. Red cedar was also used to make canoes, which were used to travel by water. Some canoes were 50 feet (15 m) long!

Red cedar trees are sometimes called the "tree of life" by tribes of the Northwest Coast. These trees give wood for strong longhouses, canoes, and art!

red cedar tree

longhouse and totem pole

Northwest Coast art also shows how tribes celebrate special occasions. Tribes commonly hold a feast when they raise a totem pole. Sometimes they're raised during a special event, called a potlatch.

Grandma says potlatches were very important occasions in a community. In the past, a family or multiple families shared their food and belongings with others to show how much they had to give. Some potlatches included special dances. Some dancers wore masks like the ones I saw before.

Potlatches are traditions that were passed down for many years. Tribes still celebrate with potlatches today.

The Importance of Art

Some pieces of art in my grandma's collection are from long ago, and some are new. That's because Northwest Coast tribes continue to make their art. Making art is a tradition that's passed down through families.

The most important thing I learned today is that art can show how people live and celebrate special occasions. Art can show where a tribe lives, what's important in their culture, and how they see the world around them. It's fun to learn about Native American cultures!

There are a few major Northwest Coast tribes. Although their art is alike, each tribe has a special style.

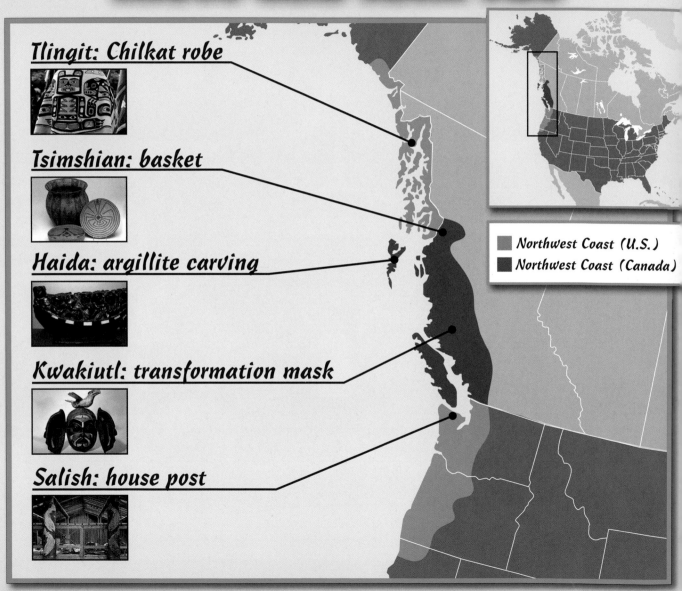

Tlingit: Chilkat robe

Tsimshian: basket

Haida: argillite carving

Kwakiutl: transformation mask

Salish: house post

Northwest Coast (U.S.)
Northwest Coast (Canada)

Glossary

culture (KUHL-chur) The language, customs, ideas, and art of a particular group of people.

folklore (FOHK-lohr) The stories of a group of people that are handed down through the years.

represent (reh-prih-ZEHNT) To stand for or be a sign of.

tradition (truh-DIH-shun) The beliefs and ways of life handed down from parents to children over many years.

transform (trans-FOHRM) To change the form, shape, character, or nature of something or someone.

Index